Contents

Introduction	V
Background	1
Allied Strategy	11
Landing Preparations	16
Ottoman Defenses	22
Gallipoli Landings	27
Anzac Cove	33
Cape Helles	37
Land and Sea	42
May 1915	46
July 1915	53
August Offensive	56

Evacuation	63
Military Consequences	70
Lessons Learned	76
Sickness and Death	81
Ensuing Operations	84
Anzac Spirit	86
Sir Ian Hamilton	89
William Birdwood	94
Otto Liman von Sanders	98
Mustafa Kemal Atatürk	103
Author's Note	106

Introduction

Gallipoli and its ill-fated campaign still resonate over a hundred years after the event. This brief campaign fought between April 1915 and January 1916 was doomed from the beginning. It has been criticized as a hopeless attempt guaranteed to do nothing but preside over an epic slaughter of its combatants.

The battle of Gallipoli was an Ottoman victory. A resounding victory that hemmed the allies into three fragments of the peninsula—leaving them unable to break out. Because of the Ottoman forces' determined soldiery, competent leadership, and intelligent use of terrain and resources on their home territory, the Allies had little choice but to retreat from the peninsula. Constantinople was never under threat.

Following this failure by the Allies, Gallipoli became a battleground of a new sort of war of words between nations seeking to blame others for what was ultimately a failure. Accusations began before the campaign was over, and reputations were destroyed. Churchill fell from grace and would serve his own time on the Western Front as a battalion commander of the Royal Scots Fusiliers. General Ian Hamilton, commander-in-chief of the military forces and one of Britain's most senior and experienced soldiers, would never again serve in a meaningful military capacity.

Like Vimy Ridge for the Canadians, Gallipoli became associated with the birth of nationhood. New Zealand and Australia emerged from behind the skirts of their mother country, and a new nation of Turkey rose from the burning ashes of the Ottoman Empire after World War One.

Gallipoli is a place of great national pride for the Turks. Their campaign was a well-executed defense of their homeland, leading to an increased memorialization of the peninsula.

INTRODUCTION

Every year, thousands of people from Australia and New Zealand crowd to the small cove on Gallipoli officially named Anzac Cove by Mustafa Kemal Atatürk (the former military commander and founding father of the Republic of Turkey) to honor their history. The limited facilities have created tensions as crowds of people have caused the erosion of the fragile surfaces, leading to a controversial new roadway cutting through the fragile battlefield terrain and exposing the bleached white bones of soldiers' remains.

The 1915 Gallipoli campaign was short. It took just over eight months and was extremely bloody. Casualties were high, as were deaths caused by illnesses because of disease and poor hygiene. The logistically challenging and poorly planned Gallipoli was a perfect example of how not to execute an amphibious landing. But without the painful and bloody lessons learned at Gallipoli, the enormity of planning the Normandy invasion of 1944 would have been even more difficult.

Many published books trace the well-worn path of discussing the Gallipoli campaign, considering the what-ifs, and drawing conclusions based on the stated ambitions. There have been accounts from both parties (though relatively little accessible work from the Ottoman side) analyzing the minutia of the campaign from its mapping to its medical preparations, original research, and even insights into many new angles. This short read is intended as an overview of some of the most critical aspects of the campaign. It's meant to be a basic introduction to the battle for a new audience.

Background

SINCE THE END OF the Crimean War in 1856, the Balkans have been in a near-constant state of turmoil. This instability was because of the dangerous state of its two oldest empires, the Austria-Hungarian Hapsburgs and the Ottoman Empire. Ripped apart by ethnic differences and new national awareness, the Balkans turned inwards on each other in 1912, creating a powder keg that would ultimately lead to the First World War.

After the assassination of Archduke Francis Ferdinand on June 28, 1914, the major European powers were now at each other's throats, and, to quote Sir Edward Grey, "The lamps are going out all over Europe."

For the Ottoman Empire, the prospect of another war was unpalatable. The young Turks who had overthrown the Sultan in 1909 had modernized the country and the military—but it still was not enough. The Ottomans were defeated in the Balkan Wars, and their European possessions were stripped to only a small part of Thrace and a sliver of land that would form the northern shore of the Dardanelles Strait.

The Dardanelles is a narrow passageway between Asian Turkey and Europe. It's a tightly constrained waterway created by geological faulting over hundreds of years. This waterway connects the strategic Aegean Sea in the Mediterranean Sea with the Sea of Marmara, through to the Bosphorus, and into the Black Sea—a point of interest for military strategists for centuries.

Constantinople (now known as Istanbul) guards the entrance to the Black Sea and controls entry to the winter Russian ports. Because of this and several other reasons, Constantinople had been coveted for hundreds of years, especially by their old enemies: Russia and Greece.

BACKGROUND

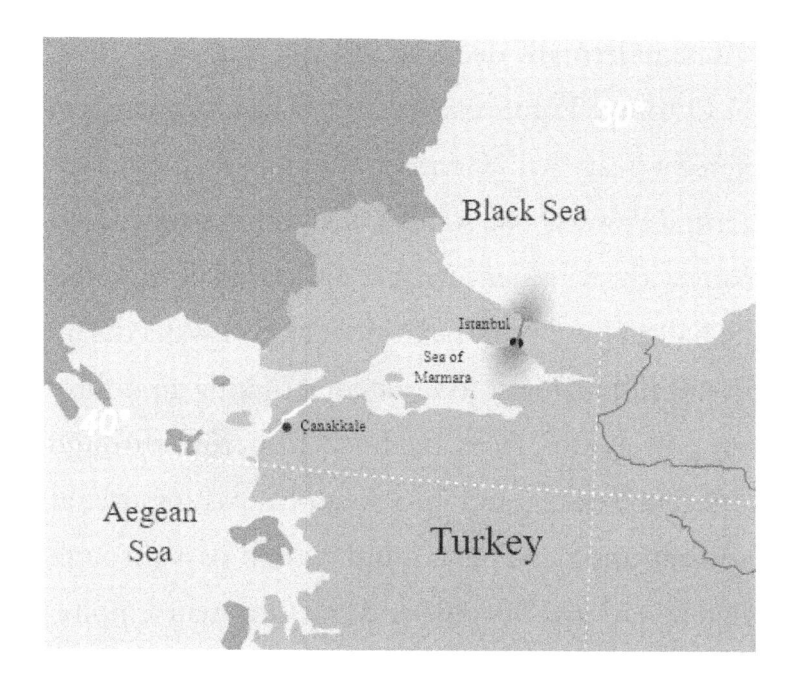

The Gallipoli Peninsula guards the Dardanelles' shores on the European side of Turkey. It's a narrow finger of land named after its first settlement, Gelibolu or Gallipoli. On the Asiatic shore, opposing this is the greater part of modern Turkey and the heart of the faltering Ottoman Empire in 1915. While fortified for centuries, the idea of squeezing ships between the tight shores of the Dardanelles had fascinated the military minds of many nations for hundreds of years.

When Germany declared war on August 4, 1914, the Ottoman Empire was neutral. The Ottomans had signed a treaty with Germany, binding them into the Central Powers. The Kaiser believed in a greater Germany with an influence that could spread throughout the Balkans and into the Middle East. It was a dream that would manifest itself in constructing an unbroken railway link from Baghdad to Berlin, through Thracian Turkey, and into Anatolia, passing over at Constantinople. This rail link would pass through aligned nations, Bulgaria and the Ottoman Empire, but had the belligerent Serbs set squarely in the way.

Germany was going to make sure its eastward enemy, Russia, was depleted in support and supplies. As most Russian war material would have to travel the southern winter route through the strait into the Black Sea, the temptation to make sure the Dardanelles were closed to traffic was significant.

German influence was already strong, from military missions into the Ottoman Empire since the late nineteenth century. Their influence would become even more pronounced when the British Admiralty (headed by Churchill), fearing the lean toward Germany, confiscated two large battleships being built by British shipyards for the Ottoman Empire.

This brought tensions to a boil on August 10 when the German warships, *Goeben* and *Breslau*, were granted passage through the supposedly neutral Dardanelles to Constantinople. These ships became symbolic substitutes for the ships stolen by the British. The final and fatal blow to British influence was the appointment of German Admiral Wilhelm Souchon to command the Ottoman navy.

With the Ottomans committed to war, the British sought to ensure they would be dispatched quickly. The British and French believed this would remove any possibility of Ottoman aggression against their possessions and protectorates in the Middle East. The Allied powers had low opinions of the strength of the Ottoman military, especially considering their defeat during the Balkan Wars.

For hundreds of years, Russia and Greece had yearned to possess the imperial city of Constantinople, which sat in ultimate control of the Black Sea route. With the Ottomans in such a weak position, the gears of diplomacy began to grind; the essential goal was to carve up what remained of the Ottoman Empire, spreading from European Thrace into the Arabian Peninsula.

First to act were the Greeks. On August 19, the British received a notice that the Greek navy and military resources were now at the disposal of the Allies.

Seizing this, the Russians approached the pro-German Greek King Constantine (married to the Kaiser's sister) and asked him to provide an expeditionary force to attack the Dardanelles. All eyes were now focused on Constantinople.

This combination of circumstances led to the evolution of the Dardanelles expedition—gradually spiraling out of control—and would consume all involved and have lasting effects on their lives. The Ottoman Empire's entry into the conflict left the Allied powers with little choice but to show their intentions that this would not be taken lightly. The Russians showed by military force that the Ottoman decision to side with the Central Powers in the upcoming conflict was unwise.

The British exercised the old concept famous in the nineteenth century of "Forcing the Dardanelles" to threaten Constantinople, especially if the Greeks could take the North Shore of the Strait of the Gallipoli Peninsula in force and if the Russians could be there to assist the Allies at Constantinople. In their minds, this would undoubtedly lead to an Ottoman surrender and remove any threat to Egypt and the Suez Canal.

At the first meeting of the war council in November 1914, Churchill reignited the Dardanelles question by suggesting that the best way to protect the Suez Canal in Egypt was to capture the Gallipoli Peninsula. He persuaded the Council that this would be possible only with naval action. This set the scene for the Gallipoli landings.

On January 3, 1915, Admiral Sir Sackville Hamilton Carden, the commander of the Eastern Mediterranean Squadron, was asked for his views on the idea of forcing the Dardanelles. Churchill, at the time, was First Sea Lord and had high hopes that the age-old naval concept of putting ships' guns against stone fortresses and forcing a passage through the Dardanelles Strait could be achieved. However, he did not know that the Dardanelles were as well defended as they were. Admiral Carden was cagey with his political masters; he replied that the Dardanelles should not be rushed. He suggested that by using extended operations with large numbers of ships, they might be forced, but he was cautious. However, the British Admiralty took this statement as a positive and requested Admiral Carden to expand on his ideas.

The admiral detailed a four-stage plan that involved reducing the forts at Seddülbahir and Kum Kale at the mouth of the Dardanelles. Then destroy the inside defenses at the entrance of the Narrows, reducing the forts at the Narrows, then finally clear the minefield, which would reduce the defenses above the Narrows and advance into the Sea of Marmara. While this plan was cautious and careful, it caught Churchill's imagination, and he believed he could execute it in theater by seeing the plan written. Admiral Carden's plan would ignite the flames.

The Admiralty decided that a combined operation was preferable to an only naval attempt, and it would be necessary for troops to follow up to secure success. The Gallipoli Peninsula and Constantinople would need to be occupied. With the Russians and Greeks

BACKGROUND

involved, there could be no doubt about the success, but there were no guarantees that any initial diplomatic advances would have any concrete proposals. Field Marshall and Secretary of State for War Lord Kitchener believed that no British troops were available other than those already committed.

Lord Kitchener was an autocrat, careful in the way of husbanding his military resources and resistant to many schemes that would widen the war on other fronts. He did not believe in diverting valuable manpower from the only front that fully engaged the Germans in Flanders. Kitchener believed the Western Front would need to come first and that attacking Gallipoli would be a costly, bloody, and lengthy campaign.

But the Admiralty believed that attempting a purely naval attempt in the Dardanelles would not be enough. Churchill stated at a war council that the Admiralty should prepare for a naval expedition in February and assault the Gallipoli Peninsula by bombardment with Constantinople as its objective.

He also hinted at the military objectives. In addition to ships, a Special Service Force of two Royal

Marine Light Infantry battalions would be reserved for Dardanelles service. They were sent to the island of Lemnos in February 1915 and used as demolition parties against batteries and forts.

This set the scene for a greater military engagement and, ultimately, the landings at Gallipoli. The momentum was now gathering.

ALLIED STRATEGY

Before the Gallipoli campaign was formed, the British had planned to carry out an amphibious assault near Alexandretta on the Mediterranean in 1914. This idea was presented to Kitchener in order to split the capital from Syria, Palestine, and Egypt. Alexandretta was the strategic center of the Ottoman railway network. Victory here would carve the Ottoman Empire in two.

East Indies commander-in-chief, Vice Admiral Richard Peirse, ordered Captain Frank Larkin of the HMS *Doris* to Alexandretta on December 13, 1914. The French cruiser *Requin* and the Russian cruiser *Askold* were both there. Kitchener had devised a plan in March 1915 to incite an Arab revolt.

The landing at Alexandretta was eventually abandoned because it would have needed more resources than France could give. Also, France did not want the British to function in their sphere of influence.

On the Western Front, by late 1914, the British and French counteroffensive at the Marne's first battle had finished. The British, French, and Belgians suffered enormous losses in the Ypres Battle in Flanders. The initial war of maneuver had ended, and now trench warfare had begun.

Austria-Hungary and the German Empire closed the overland trade routes between France, Britain, and Russia in the east. The White Sea and the Sea of Okhotsk were ice-covered in winter and distant from the Eastern Front. The Imperial German Navy had blockaded the Baltic Sea, and the Ottoman Empire controlled the entrance to the Black Sea through the Dardanelles. While the Ottomans remained neutral at this time, supplies could be sent to Russia through the Dardanelles Strait, but before the Ottomans entered the war, the strait had been closed. In November, the Ottomans mined the waterway.

The French minister of justice proposed attacking the Ottoman Empire in November, but this was rejected. An effort by the British to buy off the Ottomans also failed. Later that month, Churchill suggested a naval attack on the Dardanelles based partly on erroneous reports of Ottoman troop strength. Churchill wanted to use several obsolete battleships in the Gallipoli campaign with a limited force the army would provide. He believed an attack on the Ottomans could bring Bulgaria and Greece (formally Ottoman possessions) into the war for the Allies. In January 1915, the Russian Czar Nicholas II appealed to Britain for help against the Ottomans who were campaigning in the Caucasus.

In February 1915, a British seaplane from the HMS *Ark Royale* flew a sortie over the Dardanelles Strait. Two days later, the first attack began when an Allied task force, which included the British HMS *Queen Elizabeth*, started a long-range bombardment of the Ottoman coastal artillery batteries. The British planned to use eight aircraft from the *Ark Royale* to spot for the bombardment, but harsh weather rendered all but one of these unserviceable. The weather had slowed the initial assault, but by February 25, the outer forts had been destroyed and the entrance cleared of all mines. The Royal Marines were then landed to destroy the guns at Seddülbahir and Kum Kale, while the naval bombardment shifted to the batteries between Kephez and Kum Kale.

Churchill was frustrated by the ability of the Ottoman defenders that evaded Allied bombings and still threatened the minesweepers sent to clear the strait. Pressure was built on naval commander Admiral Carden to increase the fleet's efforts. Carden drew up new plans on March 4 and cabled Churchill, informing him the fleet would arrive in Constantinople in less than two weeks.

The sense of approaching victory was increased by the intercept of a German wireless message that revealed the Ottoman forces were running low on supplies and ammunition. Some Dardanelles forts were entirely out of ammunition. When Carden received this message, he agreed that the thrust of the attack should be launched around March 17. Before the assault, Carden suffered a stroke from the stress and was placed on the sick list. Admiral John de Robeck took over his command.

LANDING PREPARATIONS

ON THE MORNING OF March 18, 1915, an Allied fleet of eighteen battleships, destroyers, and cruisers attacked the narrowest point of the Dardanelles, where the strait was one mile wide. Despite light damage to Allied ships from the Ottoman forts' return fire, the minesweepers were ordered along the strait. According to the official Ottoman account, by 1400, all telephone wires were slashed, all communications with the forts were interrupted, and some guns had been knocked out.

Because of the artillery fire, the defense slackened significantly. The French battleship *Bouvet* hit a mine and capsized in less than two minutes. Only 75 sailors survived out of a crew of 718. Minesweepers manned by civilians retreated under Ottoman fire and left the minefields mostly intact. The HMS *Inflexible* and HMS *Irresistible* also struck mines, and the former was sank with most of her remaining crew rescued. The HMS *Inflexible* was severely damaged and forced to withdraw. During the battle, there was confusion about the damage's cause. Some accounts blame the torpedoes. The HMS *Ocean* was sent to rescue the HMS *Irresistible* but was damaged by an artillery shell before striking a mine and sinking.

French battleships *Gaulois* and *Suffren* sailed through a line of mines placed stealthily by the Ottoman minelayer *Nusret* ten days earlier and suffered significant damage. These losses forced Admiral de Robeck to withdraw and protect what remained of his force.

Some naval losses had been expected during the campaign. And, mainly, out-of-date battleships inadequate to confront the German fleet had been sent. However, a handful of senior naval officers, like Commodore Roger Keyes, commander of the *Queen Elizabeth*, felt they had come close to victory. They believed the Ottoman guns had nearly run out of ammunition, but Admiral de Robeck's views prevailed. The Allied attempts to force the strait using naval power were ended because of losses attributed to poor weather. The next step was to capture the Turkish defenses by land to open the way for the ships.

After the failed naval attacks, troops assembled to eliminate the Ottoman mobile artillery, preventing Allied minesweepers from clearing the way for larger vessels. Kitchener appointed General Ian Hamilton to lead the 78,000 men of the Mediterranean Expeditionary Force. Soldiers from the New Zealand Expeditionary Force and Australian Imperial Force were camped in Egypt, training to join the fight. The Australian and New Zealand soldiers were molded into the famous Australian and New Zealand Army Corps (ANZAC). They were commanded by General William Birdwood and comprised the volunteer 1st Australian Division and the New Zealand Division. The 29th Division and the Royal Naval Division also joined these ANZAC troops.

LANDING PREPARATIONS

The French Orient Expeditionary Corps, which initially comprised two brigades within one division, was also placed under General Hamilton's command.

Over the following month, Hamilton developed his plan for the British and French divisions and joined the Australians in Egypt. Hamilton planned to focus on the southern part of the Peninsula at Seddülbahir and Cape Helles—where an unopposed landing was expected. At first, the Allies discounted the fighting proficiency of the Ottoman soldiers. This naivety of

Allied planners was illustrated by a leaflet issued to the British and Australians still in Egypt.

"Turkish soldiers, as a rule, will surrender by holding the rifle butt upward and waving clothes or rags of any color. If an actual white flag is used, it should be regarded with suspicion, as the Turkish soldier is unlikely to have anything of that colour."

Underestimating the Ottoman military stemmed from an Allied sense of superiority because of the decay of the Ottoman Empire and its inferior performance in Libya during the war of 1911 and the Balkan Wars of 1912. This led to the Allied intelligence failure to adequately train for the campaign, and sometimes even relying on information gained from Egyptian travel guides.

The troops loaded on transports in the order they would disembark, causing a long delay. This caused many troops, including the French at Mudros, to detour into Alexandria before finding a ship that would take them to battle.

This caused a five-week delay until the end of April, during which the Ottomans strengthened their defenses on the peninsula. Poor weather in March and

LANDING PREPARATIONS

April might have delayed landings anyway, which would've prevented supply and reinforcement. After preparations in Egypt, Hamilton's headquarters staff arrived at Mudros on April 10. The ANZAC Corps left Egypt in early April. They assembled on the island of Lemnos in Greece on April 12, where a smaller garrison had been established in early March, and training for the amphibious landings was started.

The 29th British Division left for Mudros on April 7, and the Royal Naval Division trained on Skyros Island after arriving on April 17. That same day, the British submarine HMS *E15* tried to run the strait but struck a submarine net and ran aground. The sub was shelled mercilessly by the Ottomans, killing its commander and six of her crew—the survivors were forced to surrender.

On March 19, British and French troops in the Allied fleet assembled at Mudros to try again, but poor weather prevented them from making the landing and grounded Allied aircraft for nine days, restricting them to a limited schedule of reconnaissance flights.

Ottoman Defenses

The Ottomans were prepared to repel landings on either side of the strait with their 5th Army. This force comprised five divisions, with another on the way. It was a conscription force commanded by Otto Liman von Sanders. Many senior officers in the Ottoman 5th Army were German. Ottoman commanders and senior German officers discussed the best method of defending the peninsula. They agreed that the best defense was to maintain the high ground on the ridges of the peninsula. While there was disagreement about where the enemy would land and where to centralize forces, Colonel Mustafa Kemal was knowledgeable about the Gallipoli Peninsula from his operations in the Balkan Wars. He predicted that Gaba Tepe and Cape Helles (the southern tip of the peninsula) were the likely areas for an Allied landing.

Mustafa Kemal believed the British would use their naval power to control the land from every side of the peninsula's tip. This meant from Gaba Tepe, it was only a short distance to the eastern coast where the Allies could reach the Narrows (the right-angle bend in the middle of the Dardanelles).

Ottoman commanders believed Besika Bay on the Asiatic coast was most vulnerable to an invasion. The terrain was easier to cross, and the Allies could attack the Ottoman batteries guarding the strait, where a third of the 5th Army was assembled. Two divisions concentrated at the north end of the Gallipoli Peninsula at Bulair, protecting the communication and supply lines to the defenses further down the peninsula.

The 9th and 19th Divisions were placed along the Aegean coast and on the tip of the Peninsula at Cape Helles. The bulk of the Ottoman forces were inland in reserve, leaving a bare minimum of troops guarding the coast. A cavalry brigade and the 3rd Division arrived from Constantinople in early April, bringing Ottoman front-line strength to over 60,000 men. Sanders concentrated these troops into three groups. A maximum effort was ordered to improve land and sea communications and move reinforcements swiftly into threat points. Troops moved at night to bypass Allied air reconnaissance. Sanders's strategy was opposed by other Ottoman commanders, including Mustafa Kemal, who believed that the defenders were too widely spread out to defeat the invasion on the beaches. Kemal believed that Sanders's strategy was suitable when there was a strategical deepness to the front, but Gallipoli did not offer that. Sanders was confident that a rigid system of defense would fail, and the only hope of success was in the movability of his troops, mainly the 19th Division near Boghali held in reserve and ready to move to Gaba Tepe, Bulair, or the Asiatic shore.

However, the time needed by the British to organize the landings meant the Ottoman defenders had more time to prepare their defenses. The British allowed the Ottomans an additional four weeks to plan and prepare before their assault. Roads were built. Small boats were made to take troops and supplies across the Narrows, beaches were wired, and makeshift mines were built from torpedo warheads. Gun placements and trenches were dug along the beaches, and troops ran marches to avoid being lethargic.

The 19th Division under Mustafa Kemal was vital to the beaches' defenses and observed and awaited signs of an invasion from his post near Maidos. The Ottomans also created aviation squadrons with

German help and had four operating aircraft around Çanakkale.

The Ottomans conducted reconnaissance sorties from April 11 onward. Their aircraft made frequent flights over Mudros, monitoring the assembly of the British Naval Force from an airfield they established near Gallipoli.

Gallipoli Landings

In April 1915, The Allies intended to land and secure the northern shore of Gallipoli. They planned to capture the Ottoman forts and artillery batteries so a fleet could sail through to the Narrows and the Sea of Marmara toward Constantinople.

Initially scheduled for April 23 but postponed until the 25th because of bad weather, the landings were planned to take place at five beaches on the peninsula. The 29th would land at the tip of the peninsula at Helles, then advance on the forts at Kilitbahir. The 3rd Australian Infantry Brigade, the ANZACs, spearheading the assault, would land north of Gaba Tepe on the Aegean coast, where they would cut off the Ottoman troops in Kilitbahir by advancing across the peninsula and stopping reinforcements from reaching Cape Helles.

This sector of the Gallipoli Peninsula would be known as Anzac Cove. The area held by the French and British became known as the Helles. The French had made a diversionary landing on the Asian shore at Kum Kale before re-embarking to secure the eastern area of the Helles sector.

Naval gunfire support for the landings had initially included bombarding the beaches and approaches. In reality, it was changed to engaging the ridges around the landings, with only the beaches to be shelled before the landings. No decision was made about the issue of close support, and instead left to the discretion of the ships' captains. A hesitancy to approach the shore later affected the landings at Beaches V and W. This was where some of the worst losses among the infantry occurred. Naval gunfire supported landing troops at Beaches S, X, and Anzac Cove. But even then, the effectiveness could have been improved by the initial onshore confusion, broken terrain, thick vegetation, and lack of observation.

Kitchener had ruled that the Royal Naval Air Service must meet air requirements, and the Allies employed a small force of seaplanes and other aircraft from the RNAS, which arrived at the end of March. The squadron was unchallenged at first by the small Ottoman Air Force. The Allies' small force of aircraft had been used to provide aerial surveillance, although it eventually proved incompetent to meet the intelligence the Allies needed to make up for the lack of adequate maps. After the landings, Allied aircraft carried out photographic surveillance, observed naval gunfire, reported on Ottoman troop movements, and conducted several bombing raids.

General Birdwood's ANZAC troops numbered over 25,000 men at the northern landing. This force would be the first on the beach and cut the communications to the Ottoman forces in the south. The 3rd Infantry Brigade would be the covering force and advance inland to establish positions on Gun

Ridge. The 2nd Infantry Brigade would follow and capture higher ground on Sari Bair. The 1st Infantry Brigade would be the last to land and act as the division's reserve. The main ANZAC force would assemble at night and execute a dawn landing surprising the defenders on the evening of April 24. The covering force embarked on destroyers and battleships with follow-on forces and transports. Troops were to disembark from the transports and the ships' boats. Then, they'd be hauled close to shore by steamboats before rowing ashore.

At 0200, an Ottoman observer reported multiple ships on the horizon. A captain in charge of the company from the 27th Infantry Regiment confirmed the sighting with his binoculars and informed his commanding officer at Kabatepe.

By 0300, the moon was covered, and the ships weren't detectable. The Ottomans weren't sure if this was an actual landing or diversion. Once powerful artillery was heard at around 0600, two battalions of the 27th Infantry Regiment were urgently ordered to make their way to Ariburnu. Limon von Sanders had left his headquarters and was at Bulair with the

Ottoman 5th Division, waiting for the actual landing. His absence created problems in the chain of command and delays in decision-making, which negated his defense scheme that relied on rapid troop movement.

At 0400 on the morning of April 25, the first wave of troops from the 3rd Brigade began moving towards the shore on ships' boats. The covering force landed approximately 2 km too far north and ended up in a bay south of Ari Burnu. Because of undetected currents or navigational error, the landing was on ground that rose steeply from the beaches, unlike the southern aim, which was more open. Only two Ottoman companies garrisoned the landing site. However, they held the high ground and inflicted considerable casualties on the Australians before being overtaken. The jagged terrain hampered a coordinated drive inland.

The Australians were on unfamiliar ground and used inaccurate maps. In the maze of dense scrub, spurs, and steep ravines, Australian parties that lost contact were reorganized into smaller groups. While some Australian troops reached the second ridge, only a few reached their objectives. The rest had become scattered. The covering force provided little support for the follow-up force.

Anzac Cove

On April 25, the 1st and 2nd Brigades, followed by the New Zealand and Australian Divisions, landed on the beaches around Ari Burnu. But they got entangled, and it took over four hours after the landing began to sort them out. By then, the bulk of the 1st Australian Division was ashore safely. Its leading elements were pushing inland by midmorning. Kemal had reorganized the defenders for a counterattack on the commanding heights of Sari Bair.

BROOKES SERIES — THE LANDING AT ANZAC — GALLIPOLI
25th APRIL 1915

The right flank of a small beachhead taken by the Australians was repelled at 1030, with most of 400 Plateau being lost. During the afternoon, the left flank was forced back from Baby 700. By evening, Birdwood believed (after information from the navy) that embarkation was impossible and ordered the troops to dig in. The Ottoman counterattack eventually was repulsed, and the Australians established a perimeter roughly from northern Walkers Ridge to Shell Green in the south. ANZAC casualties on the first day numbered over 2,000 men. Failure to take the high ground caused a tactical stalemate, and the defenders contained the landings in a perimeter less than two kilometers.

The Australian submarine HMAS *AE2* penetrated the strait on the night of April 24. As the landings began at Cape Helles and Anzac Cove at dawn on April 25, the submarine reached Chanak at 0600, torpedoed a Turkish gunboat, and evaded a destroyer. The Australian submarine then ran aground beneath the Ottoman fort, but the gunners failed to turn their guns quickly enough, and the *AE2* maneuvered safely away. Shortly after she floated away, her periscope was sighted by an Ottoman battleship firing over the Allied landing sites. The *AE2* advanced toward the Sea of Marmara at 0830 and waited on the seabed until nightfall.

At 2100, the *AE2* surfaced to recharge batteries and send a wireless report to the fleet. The message detailed how the landing at Cape Helles was proceeding well, but Anzac Cove was unsuccessful, and Birdwood contemplated the re-embarkation of his troops. The success of this Australian submarine was a consideration for Birdwood's decision to persist.

Reports of the sub's exploits improved the soldiers' morale. The *AE2* was given orders to "generally run amok." With no enemies in sight, she sailed into the Sea of Marmara, where she operated for five days, attacking Ottoman ships.

Cape Helles

The 29th Division landed on five beaches around the tip of Cape Helle's peninsula. They were known as S, V, W, X, and Y Beaches, laid out strategically from east to west.

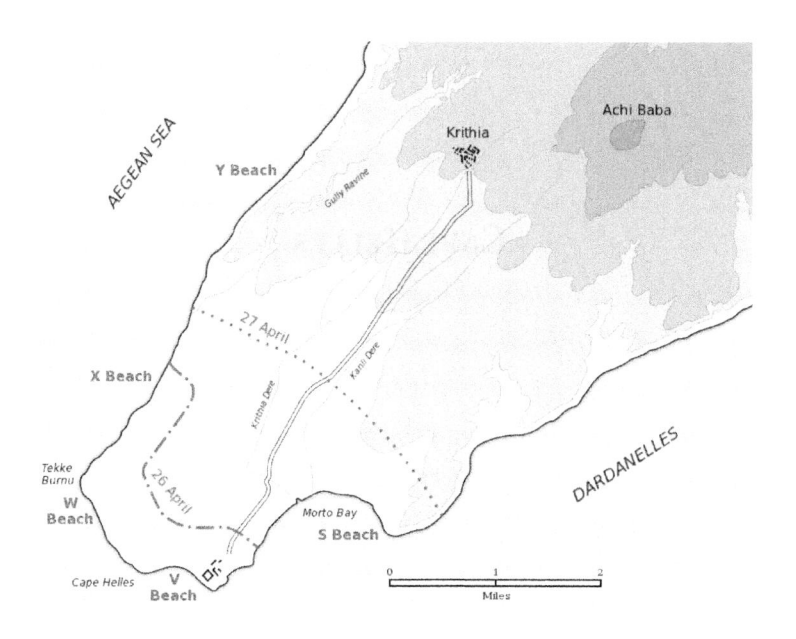

On May 1, the 29th Indian Brigade landed and took Sari Bair above the landing beaches; the 5th and 10th Gurkha Rifles and the Zion Mule Corps joined them. At Y Beach, during the first engagement at the Battle of Krithia. The Allies landed unopposed and advanced inland. There were few Ottoman defenders in the village. But without orders to advance their position, the commander at Y Beach withdrew his force back to the beachhead. This was the closest the Allies would come to capturing the village. The Ottomans quickly brought up a battalion of the 25th Regiment to stop any further advance.

V Beach was where the main landing was made, under the fortress of the old Seddülbahir. Landings were also made at W Beach, on the other side of the headland to the west. A covering force of Royal Munster Fusiliers was landed from a converted coal transport ship, the SS *River Clyde*, which ran aground beneath the fortress so the soldiers could debark along ramps. The Royal Dublin Fusiliers disembarked at V Beach, while the Lancashire Fusiliers landed at W Beach using open boats onto a shore obstructed with barbed wire and overlooked by dunes.

On both beaches, Ottoman troops held strong defensive positions and caused several casualties to Allied landing troops. Machine gunners shot soldiers emerging one by one from ports on the *River Clyde* at Seddülbahir fort. Out of the first 200 men to land, only 21 reached the beach.

The Ottoman defenders did not have enough manpower to overwhelm the landing, but they inflicted considerable casualties and contained the attack close to shore. By the morning of April 25, the Ottomans were out of ammunition and had only bayonets to meet the Allies' troops. They fought fearlessly on the slopes that led up from the beach to the ridge of Chunuk Bair. The 57th Infantry Regiment received orders from Mustafa Kemal, ordering them to fight and die, giving other troops and commanders time to come forward and take their places. Every man of that regiment was wounded or killed.

At W Beach, known afterward as Lancashire Landing, the Lancashires overwhelmed the Ottoman defenders despite taking 600 casualties out of 1,000 men. The Lancashires earned six Victoria Crosses at W Beach, with another six awarded to troops at the V Beach landing. Another three were awarded over the following days as they fought inland. Five squads of Ottoman infantry distinguished themselves by repelling several attacks from their hilltop position. The Ottomans eventually disengaged under the cover of darkness.

After the landing, so few men remained from the Munster and Dublin Fusiliers that they were merged into the Dubsters. Only one Dublin Fusilier officer survived the landing. Out of the 1,012 Dubliners who landed, only 11 survived the Gallipoli campaign unscathed. After the landings, there was little done by the Allies to advance their position, apart from a few small thrusts inland by small groups of men. The Allied attack lost momentum, allowing the Ottomans time to bring up reinforcements and rally the small number of defending troops.

Land and Sea

Six battalions of the 5th Division reinforced the 19th Division to strengthen the Ottoman counterattack at Anzac on the afternoon of April 27. With naval gunfire support, the Allies held back the Ottomans during the night. The next day, French troops transferred to the right of the line near S Beach and joined the fight. On April 28, the Allied forces fought the First Battle of Krithia and captured the village. The Ottomans halted the Allied advance halfway between Krithia and the Helles headland around 1800, causing over 3,000 casualties.

With the arrival of Ottoman reinforcements, the potential of a quick Allied victory on the peninsula evaporated, and the fighting at Anzac and Helles became a battle of attrition. On April 30, the Royal Naval Division landed, believing the Allies were on the verge of defeat, and moved eight troops forward through a gully near the Lone Pine and 400 Plateau. Eight battalions of reinforcements were sent from Constantinople a day later.

On that afternoon, Ottoman troops counterattacked at Anzac and Helles. The Ottomans momentarily broke through to the French sector, but the attacks were repelled by Allied machine gun fire, which inflicted severe casualties on the Ottoman attackers. General Birdwood ordered the New Zealand and Australian divisions to attack. The Australian 4th Infantry Brigade and the New Zealand Infantry Brigade, along with the Royal Marines, took part in the attack. They were covered by an artillery and naval barrage. While the troops advanced a short distance through the night, they became separated in the dark. The attackers came under fierce small arms fire from their vulnerable left flank and were repelled—suffering over 1,000 casualties.

On April 30, the submarine *AE2* rose uncontrollably, surfaced near an Ottoman torpedo boat, dropped below the safe diving depth, and broke the surface again at the stern. An Ottoman torpedo boat fired on the *AE2* and punctured her pressure hull. The crew was ordered to abandon ship; the sub was scuttled, and the crew taken prisoner.

The *AE2's* achievement showed it was plausible to force the straits, and soon British and French operations badly disrupted Ottoman communications. On April 27, HMS *E14* entered the Marmara Sea on a three-week patrol. It became one of the campaign's most successful Allied naval actions, sinking four ships, including the transport *Gul Djemal*, carrying 6,000 troops into the fight for Gallipoli. The amount and value of the ships sunk was minor, but the results on Ottoman communications and morale were significant. After the success of *E14* and *AE2*, a French sub named *Joule* tried the passage on May 1 but hit a mine and went down with all hands.

May 1915

On May 5, the Allies dispatched the 42nd Division from Egypt. Believing Anzac Cove to be secure, Hamilton brought the Australian 2nd Infantry Brigade and New Zealand Infantry Brigade, along with twenty field guns, to the Helles front as reserves for the upcoming second battle of Krithia. The Allies were using a force of 20,000 men, and the first general attack on Helles was planned for daylight. French troops were ordered to capture Kereves Dere, while the British, New Zealand, and Australians were assigned Achi Baba and Krithia. After thirty minutes of artillery bombardment, the assault began midmorning on May 6. The French and British advanced along Fir Tree, Krithia, Gully, and Kereves spurs, separated by deep gullies and fortified by the Ottomans. As the attackers advanced, they got separated when trying to outflank the Ottomans, finding themselves in unfamiliar terrain. Under artillery and machine gun fire from Ottoman outposts, they had not been spotted by British aerial surveillance, and the attack was stopped.

Four battalions of New Zealanders attacked up Krithia Spur on May 7. The 29th Division reached a position south of the village before dusk. The Australian 2nd Brigade quickly advanced over open ground to the British front line. Through fierce small arms and artillery fire, the Brigade charged toward Krithia and gained 600 m (just 400 m short of the objective) while taking over 1,000 casualties.

The New Zealanders could link up with the Australians, but the British were held up, and the French were exhausted, despite occupying a point overlooking their objective. The attack was suspended after failing to take Achi Baba or Krithia, forcing the Allies to dig in.

The Allies were nearly out of ammunition, especially since the artillery on both sides merged their defenses. The Ottomans relieved troops opposing the Australian line, reinforced by the Australian Light Horse operating now as infantry. Erratic fighting persisted with sniping, grenade attacks, and raids. The opposing trenches were separated by only a few meters. The Australians lost several officers to sniping, including the commander of the 1st Division, Major

MAY 1915

General William Bridges, who was wounded while inspecting a Light Horse Regiment position. He died from his injuries on the hospital ship HMHS *Gascon*.

At the end of April, General Birdwood told GHQ (General Headquarters) that he couldn't land six thousand horses at Anzac Cove because there was no water for them. GHQ was disappointed that the Anzac force would be immobile on the beachhead. Even so, they would have been of no use. Thousands of men and their horses stayed on board the ships for almost a month.

Birdwood signaled the transports would return to Alexandria and offload over 3,000 men and 5,000 horses. Headquarters insisted some men remain in Alexandria to look after the horses and guard the ANZAC's many vehicles and mountains of baggage.

On May 19, 42,000 Ottoman troops launched an attack at Anzac Cove to smash the 17,000 New Zealanders and Australians back into the sea. While short on ammunition and artillery, the Ottomans planned on surprise and strength in numbers.

On May 18, the crew of a British aircraft spotted the Ottoman soldiers and relayed the information to

Allied planners. When the Ottomans attacked, the Allies were waiting. The Ottoman assault was a failure at a cost of 13,000 casualties, with over 3,000 men killed. The butchers' bill for the Australian and New Zealanders was 160 killed and 480 wounded. One of the dead was a stretcher bearer named John Simpson Kirkpatrick, whose efforts to evacuate wounded men on a donkey while under fire became famous among the Australians. After the war, his story became a legend in the Australian narrative of the campaign.

The Ottoman losses were so severe that a truce was organized to bury the dead laying in No Man's Land. This led to a camaraderie between the armies, like the Christmas truce on the Western Front in 1914.

According to an eyewitness account from Private Laidlaw of the Australian 2nd Field Ambulance: "The armistice was declared 8:30 a.m. this morning until 4:30 p.m.; it was wonderful. Things were so unnaturally quiet I felt like getting up and making a row myself. The rifle fire was quiet; there was no shell fire. The stench from the trenches where the dead had been lying for weeks was something awful. Some bodies were mere skeletons. It seems so very different to see each side near each other's trenches bearing their dead. Each man that took part in the ceremony was called a pioneer and wore two white bands on their arms. Everyone is also taking advantage of the armistice to do anything they want to do out of covering. A large number of men are down bathing. You think today was Cup Day down at one of our seaside beaches."

The British advantage in naval artillery dwindled after the battleship HMS *Goliath* was torpedoed on May 13 by an Ottoman destroyer. German submarine *U-21* sank the HMS *Triumph* on May 25 and HMS *Majestic* on May 27. More British surveillance patrols were flown around Gallipoli, forcing the *U-21* to leave the area. The Allies shifted several ships to Imbros, where they were protected between sorties, significantly reducing Allied naval firepower, particularly in the Helles sector. The sub HMS *E11* passed through the Dardanelles on May 18. It sank or disabled eleven ships, including three on May 23, before entering Constantinople Harbor. The *E11* also fired on a transport near the arsenal and sank a gunboat, damaging the pier.

The Ottoman forces were short of artillery, ammunition, and field batteries. They could only fire 18,000 shells between May and the first week of June. After the defeat of the Ottoman counter-attack at Anzac Cove in mid-May, Ottoman forces ceased all frontal assaults. Toward the end of the month, the Ottomans began tunneling in the ANZAC sector early on May 29, despite Australian counter-mining detonating a mine and attacking with troops from the 14th Regiment. The Australian 15th Battalion was repelled but counter-attacked, recapturing the ground before being relieved by New Zealand troops. ANZAC operations in early June returned to minor engagements and skirmishing with grenades and sniper fire.

July 1915

In the Helles sector, both sides were entrenched. On June 4, the Allies attacked Achi Baba and Krithia with the 29th Royal Naval Division, the 42nd Division, and two French divisions. This attack was repelled and with it, the possibility of any decisive breakthrough ended. Trench warfare resumed, with the objectives calculated in tens of yards.

Casualties were appalling on both sides. The French lost 2,000 men out of 10,000. Out of 20,000 troops, the British lost 4,500. The Ottoman losses were over 9,000 casualties.

In June, the carrier HMS *Ben-my-Chree* arrived, increasing the Allied air effort. The 52nd Division landed at Helles to prepare for the Battle of Gully Ravine, beginning on June 28 and successfully advancing the British line along the left flank of the battlefield. On June 30, French commander Henri Gouraud was injured and replaced by his divisional commander. In the first week of July, the Ottomans counter-attacked the new Allied line multiple times but failed to regain the lost ground. Ottoman casualties mounted and were estimated at 14,000 men. On July 2, two brigades from the 52nd Division attacked at the center of the line along Bloody Valley (Achi Baba Nullah) and gained very little ground, taking 2,500 casualties out of 7,500 men. The Royal Naval Division suffered 600 casualties, and French losses were over 800 men. Ottoman losses were around 9,000 casualties and 600 prisoners.

At sea, the submarine *E14* was active in the Sea of Marmara. On July 21, the *E14* forced her way through the strait despite a new anti-submarine net near the Narrows. On July 27, the *E14* got caught in the net, forced to the surface, and shelled by shore batteries. She was scuttled, but before that, she torpedoed the battleship *Barbaros Hayreddin*, causing the loss of 253 men and sinking a gunboat, seven transports, and twenty-three sailing vessels.

August Offensive

The Allied failure to capture Krithia and the Helles front stalemate led Hamilton to create a new plan. The general intended to secure the range of hills and capture the high ground on Hill 971 in the battles of Sari Bair and Chunuk Bair.

By now, both sides had been reinforced. The original five Allied divisions were increased to fifteen, and the first six Ottoman divisions were now at sixteen. The Allies were going to land two fresh infantry divisions from IX Corps at Suvla, just eight miles north of Anzac.

These troops would be used in an offensive against the Sari Bair range by advancing through thinly defended terrain north of the perimeter around Anzac. The Allies could attack Baby 700 by dismounting Australian Light Horsemen. This would coincide with an attack on Chunuk Bair by troops from the New Zealander Infantry Brigade who would traverse Rhododendron Ridge. The 29th Indian Brigade Gurkhas would attack Hill 971 along with the Australian 4th Infantry Brigade.

The Allies had forty aircraft, against the Ottomans' twenty planes, of which eight were stationed at Çanakkale. Allied aircraft spotted for naval guns, made reconnaissance flights, and carried out the low-level bombing of Ottoman reserve forces as they were brought up onto the battlefield. Allied aircraft also undertook shipping operations in the Gulf of Saros, where they sank an Ottoman tug with an air-launched torpedo.

On August 6, the Suvla Bay landings took place against light opposition. The British commander, General Frederick Stopford, limited his early objectives and failed to push his advance far enough inland and seized little more than the beachhead.

The Ottomans occupied the Anafarta Hills and prevented the British from penetrating inland, effectively containing the landings and reducing the front at Suvla to destructively static trench warfare. The Allied offensive proceeded on the same evening of August 6 by diversionary attacks at Helles, with the battle of Krithia Vineyard becoming another costly stalemate.

The 1st Australian Infantry Brigade led the Battle of Lone Pine and captured the main Ottoman trench line. It diverted Ottoman forces, but the attacks at Hill 971 and Chunuk Bair were miserable failures.

The New Zealanders came within 500 m of the Chunuk Bair summit on August 7. Still, they could only seize the summit the following morning. On the morning of August 7, the Australian 3rd Light Horse Brigade attacked a narrow front coinciding with the New Zealand attack against the rear of the Ottoman defenses. The opening artillery barrage was lifted seven minutes too soon, and the Australian 4th Infantry Brigade, along with an Indian Gurkha Brigade, got lost during the night. The attack on Hill 971 never happened.

Ottoman defenders repelled Allied attempts to renew their attack at a significant cost to the Allied forces; the New Zealanders could hold out at Chunuk Bair for two days before being reinforced, but an Ottoman counterattack on August 10 led by Mustafa Kemal swept through them from the heights.

Seven hundred and eleven men from the New Zealand Wellington Battalion who reached the summit were casualties out of 760. After the Ottomans recaptured the ground, the possibility of an Allied victory was lost.

Just before the evacuation at Anzac Cove, troops from the new Australian 2nd Division arrived from Egypt, with the 5th Infantry Brigade in tow. The 29th Division was moved from Helles to Suvla. The British made another attempt to resurrect their offensive on August 21 in the Battles of Scimitar Hill and Hill 60. If they had taken control of the hills, they would have united the Anzac Cove and Suvla fronts, but their attacks failed. On August 17, Hamilton requested another hundred thousand troops, but a day earlier, the French announced their plans for an autumn offensive in France to Kitchener. This led to a meeting of the Dardanelles committee on August 20, which determined the French offensive would be supported by a maximum Allied effort, leaving only about 25,000 reinforcements available for the Dardanelles.

On August 23, after news of the failed attack on Scimitar Hill, Hamilton went on to the defensive as Bulgaria entered the war, allowing the Germans to rearm the Turkish army and leaving little opportunity for resuming any offensive operations. On September 20, the Newfoundland Regiment was deployed along with the 29th Division.

On September 25, Kitchener proposed attaching two British and one French Division for service in Greece at Salonika. This spelled the beginning of the end of the Allies' campaign in Gallipoli.

Hamilton withdrew the 10th Irish Division and 156th Infantry Division, and by the end of September, these troops were mustering at Mudros for deployment to the new French front.

During this impasse, an old Ottoman batman (personal servant assigned to an officer) could hang his platoon's laundry on the barbed wire undisturbed. Also, gifts were being exchanged across No Man's Land—sweets and dates from the Ottomans and packs of cigarettes and cans of beef from the Allies. Conditions at Gallipoli grew worse for everyone.

The intense summer heat and pitiful sanitation caused an explosion in the fly population. It became difficult to eat, as unburied corpses were putrid and bloated. Allied troops were in perilous positions because they were poorly situated, and this caused shelter and supply problems. A dysentery epidemic spread like wildfire through the ANZAC trenches at

Helles and caused terrible suffering and disease, along with numerous deaths on both sides.

Evacuation

After the disappointment of the August offensive, the Gallipoli campaign began to crumble. The Ottoman successes affected public opinion in Britain, and reporters like Keith Murdoch and Ellis Bartlett smuggled out criticism of Hamilton's performance. Other officers contributed to the air of doom and gloom and raised the possibility of evacuation on October 11, 1915.

Hamilton opposed the idea. He feared the damage it could cause to British prestige but was replaced shortly afterward by General Charles Monro. The Ottoman winter eased the brutal heat but led to flooding, gales, and blizzards. This resulted in thousands of men suffering from frostbite and death from drowning and freezing. The defeat of the Serbians in the autumn of 1915 prompted Britain and France to transfer troops from the Gallipoli campaign into Greek Macedonia. This would open a Macedonian front helping what was left of the Serbian army to conquer Macedonia.

On September 4, the submarine HMS *E7* got caught in an Ottoman anti-submarine net as it began another tour. Despite these reverses, by mid-September, Allied mines and nets had closed off the eastern entrance of the Dardanelles to German U-boats. The U-21 was thwarted when it tried to pass through the strait on September 13. The first French sub to enter the Sea of Marmara was called the *Turquoise* and was forced to turn back on October 30. When the French sub returned to the Dardanelles Strait, she ran aground beneath an Ottoman fort and was captured intact. Her crew of twenty-five was taken prisoner along with documents detailing planned Allied operations, including a scheduled rendezvous on November 6. This rendezvous was kept by the German *U-14*, which torpedoed and sank the HMS *E20*, killing most of her crew.

EVACUATION

The Gallipoli situation was only made worse by Bulgaria joining the Central Powers. By October 1915, the French and British opened a second Mediterranean front at Salonika by moving two divisions out of Gallipoli and reducing the flow of reinforcements. This opened a land route between the Ottoman Empire and Germany through Bulgaria. The Germans could now rearm the Ottomans with heavy artillery to devastate the Allies' trenches, especially on the Anzac front.

At the end of November, an Ottoman crew in a German Albatross C1 modern aircraft shot down a French plane over Gaba Tepe. More Central Powers artillery units arrived, substantially reinforcing the Ottoman artillery. General Monro recommended evacuation to Kitchener, who visited the eastern Mediterranean in early November. After consulting with the commanders at Helles, Suvla, and Anzac, Kitchener agreed with Monro and sent his proposal to the British cabinet, confirming the decision to evacuate in early December.

Because of the terrain on No Man's Land and the icy winter weather, casualties were expected during this withdrawal. The pure untenable nature of Allied positions was made apparent by a rainstorm in late November 1915. The Suvla downpour continued for three days before turning into a blizzard in early December. This caused rain to flood trenches, drowning soldiers and washing unburied corpses into the lines.

Anzac and Suvla were evacuated in late December, with the last troops leaving before the sun came up on December 20. Troop numbers had slowly been reduced since early December. But the Allied troops left the Ottomans tricky booby traps to contend with. There were self-firing rifles rigged to fire by water dropping into a pan attached to the trigger. This ruse was used to trick the Ottoman troops during the Allied departure.

At Anzac Cove, the troops maintained silence for over an hour until curious Ottoman troops ventured into inspect the trenches where the ANZACs opened fire. Incidents of this nature discouraged the Ottomans from getting too close to the trenches when the actual evacuation began. The Allied force completed their withdrawal, with the Australians suffering no casualties on the final nights, but large quantities of stores and supplies fell into Ottoman hands.

Helles was kept for a short while, but GHQ's decision to evacuate the garrison was made on December 28. Unlike evacuating from Anzac, Ottoman forces looked for signs of withdrawal. Using a lull in the action to bring up supplies and reinforcements, Sanders launched an attack on the British at Gully Spur on January 7 with infantry and artillery, but the attack failed. Mines were placed with time fuses, and that night on January 7, under cover of naval bombardment, the British troops withdrew five miles to the beachhead, where makeshift piers were used to board boats. British troops departed from Lancashire, landing around midmorning on January 8.

The rearguard Newfoundland Regiment withdrew on January 9. The first to land was the rest of the Plymouth Battalion, while the Royal Marine Light Infantry was the last to leave the Gallipoli Peninsula.

Despite predictions of over 30,000 casualties, 35,268 troops with 3,689 horses and mules, 127 guns, 328 vehicles, and 1,600 tons of equipment were removed. Over 500 mules that couldn't be embarked were killed so they did not fall into Ottoman hands, and over 1,500 vehicles were left behind with smashed wheels. As at Anzac Cove, many supplies, including six unserviceable French artillery pieces, were destroyed.

Ammunition and gun carriages were left behind, and hundreds of horses were butchered to deny them to the Ottomans. A British soldier was killed by debris from a premature magazine explosion. Shortly after dawn, the Ottomans retook Helles.

During the last days of the Gallipoli campaign, a German fighter squadron increased the Ottoman air defenses. It caused the first British flying losses after the Helles evacuation when three Eindeckers shot down two RNAS aircrafts.

Military Consequences

Many will remember the Gallipoli campaign as a closely fought struggle that ultimately ended as a defeat for the Allies. In contrast, others will view the overall result as nothing but a tactical stalemate. Another observation of this campaign is that the Ottoman forces held the Allies back from the actual objective with relative ease. Some could view it as an absolute disaster for the Allies. However, the campaign caused enormous damage to Ottoman national resources.

In 1915, the Allies could replenish their troops and supplies better than the Ottomans. But in the end, the Allied effort to secure a passage through the Dardanelles failed miserably.

MILITARY CONSEQUENCES

The Allies successfully diverted Ottoman forces away from other Middle East conflict areas. The Gallipoli campaign consumed valuable resources the Allies could've employed on the Western Front, but this also resulted in heavy losses on the Central Powers side.

The Allied campaign was plagued by poor planning, insufficient artillery, poorly defined goals, inaccurate maps, poor intelligence, inexperienced troops, inadequate equipment, overconfidence, and tactical and logistical deficiencies at all levels (to name a few).

While geography also proved a significant factor, the Allied forces possessed inaccurate intelligence and faulty maps that couldn't help them use the terrain to their advantage. Ottoman commanders employed the high ground around the Allied landing beaches by positioning capable defenses that stopped the Allied forces' ability to penetrate inland. This confined them to narrow beaches. This campaign's necessity for the war's overall goal remains controversial. The accusations of negligence that followed were so significant they highlighted the division that had developed between military planners who believed the Allies should focus on the Western Front and those who favored trying to end the war by attacking Germany's soft underbelly—its allies to the east.

During the Gallipoli campaign, French and British submarine operations in the Sea of Marmara were one area of success. The sub-operations forced the Ottomans to abandon the sea as a transportation route from April 1915 to the end of 1915. British submarines sank 5 gunboats, 11 troop transports, 1 destroyer, 1 battleship, 148 sailing vessels, and 44 supply ships at the cost of only eight Allied subs sank in the straight or the Marmara Sea.

In October 1915, nine Allied subs were active in the Mediterranean following the evacuation of Helles. The Ottoman navy was forced to stop all area operations, while merchant shipping was also significantly curtailed. If the communication sea lines had been severed, the Ottoman 5th Army would have faced a catastrophe.

These operations were a source of grave concern. They posed a constant threat to shipping and caused heavy losses, effectively stopping Ottoman troops intending to reinforce their forces at Gallipoli and shelling railways and troop concentrations.

Gallipoli marked the end of Hamilton's career. The competence of Australian brigade commanders Harry Chauvel and John Monash was recognized, and they were promoted to core command positions. Kitchener's influence dwindled after the May 1915 coalition government was formed. A growing sense of failure in the Gallipoli campaign culminated in Kitchener being overruled on advising for French support at Salonika in December 1915.

The fight for Gallipoli emboldened the Ottomans' belief that they could defeat the Allied forces. In Mesopotamia, the Turks encircled a British force at Kut Al Amara, causing them to surrender in April 1916. Ottoman forces in southern Palestine were confident about launching an attack against Egypt and the Suez Canal. Their defeat at the Battle of Romani and the lack of supplies to complete the military railway necessary for such an upward operation marked the end of that ambition.

The optimism gained by the Ottomans from the triumph at Gallipoli was swapped for a sense of despair as the British kept on the Middle East offensive for the rest of the war.

Lessons Learned

Gallipoli's amphibious operations were studied by military planners and influenced other amphibious campaigns like Normandy in 1944 and the Falklands in 1982. Gallipoli's lessons learned influenced the US Marine Corps' amphibious operations doctrine during the Pacific War in World War Two. The Gallipoli campaign became a well-studied subject as it related to amphibious warfare in the United States and Britain. Gallipoli had all four types of amphibious operations: demonstration, raid, assault, and withdrawal.

LESSONS LEARNED

Analyzing the Gallipoli campaign before the outbreak of World War Two, it was believed that amphibious assaults would fail against modern defenses. Even despite the landings in Tarawa, Italy, and the Gilbert Island chains, this perception continued until June 1944 at Normandy.

The invasion of Normandy proved opposed landings were possible with proper planning. Gallipoli's memory weighed upon the Australians during the planning of the 1943 Huon Peninsula campaign. In September, Australians made the first opposed amphibious landing since Gallipoli at the Finschhafen battle in New Guinea. Navigational errors caused troops to land ashore on the wrong beaches, but they were still trained according to Gallipoli's lessons and quickly reorganized, pushing inland.

The political repercussions in Britain had begun during the battle. The uproar following Conservatives learning that Churchill would stay forced Prime Minister Herbert Asquith to end his liberal government and to form a coalition government with the Conservative Party.

The Asquith government responded to the failure and fury over Gallipoli by setting up an inquiry commission. A Dardanelles commission was set up to investigate the expedition's failure. The first report was issued in 1917 and published in 1919, following the failure of the Gallipoli campaign.

General Hamilton was recalled to London in October, ending his military career. Churchill resigned in November 1915 and took command of an infantry battalion on the Western Front.

Asquith was partially blamed for Gallipoli. He was ousted in December 1916 when David Lloyd George proposed a war council under his authority. The

Conservatives in the coalition threatened to resign unless this plan was implemented. After failing to reach an agreement, Asquith resigned and David Lloyd George became prime minister.

Lloyd George formed a new government. In the summer of 1917, Churchill was appointed to the cabinet as the minister of munitions—not to the war cabinet.

The commission's eventual report was published in 1919. It concluded that Hamilton was over-optimistic from the beginning and had added to the difficulties. Hamilton emerged from the investigation more favorably than perhaps was justified. Partly because he tried to conspire with witnesses and got leaked reports from the commission's deliberations. Hamilton was never given another appointment.

Casualty figures for the Gallipoli campaign vary between sources. According to a study published in 2001, over 100,000 men were killed, with 56,000 Ottoman and 53,000 British and French soldiers. Using the Turkish archives, it's estimated that Ottoman casualties in the Gallipoli campaign were 56,000 men dead, 97,000 troops wounded, and 11,000 missing or captured. British General John Maxwell stated, "The appetite of the Dardanelles for men has been wicked and phenomenal."

There were over half a million casualties during the Gallipoli campaign. The British history of the Great War lists the casualties as over 205,000 British, 47,000 French, and 251,000 Ottoman troops. (Modern-day Turkish sources refer to these casualties much higher at 350,000.)

According to New Zealand semiofficial history, there were about 16,500 New Zealanders that served at Gallipoli, with about 251,000 Ottoman battle casualties, including 86,000 dead. Over 2,800 New Zealanders were killed, and about a quarter of those who disembarked on Gallipoli were wounded. Other estimates show an even higher amount of New Zealand soldiers serving at Gallipoli, with over 16,000 and nearly 9,000 dead.

SICKNESS AND DEATH

The unsanitary conditions led to many soldiers becoming sick from typhoid, dysentery, and diarrhea. It was reported that over 90,000 British soldiers were evacuated for sickness during the campaign. Over 150,000 British troops fell sick, not counting Indian or Colonial troops. Of these, 3,800 died. The sick were conveyed from Gallipoli to hospitals in Malta and Egypt as quickly as possible because the bases in the area of operations were insufficient.

The portion of disease casualties to battle casualties was much higher in the Gallipoli campaign than in the Western Front campaigns. Approximately 3% of men removed as non-battle casualties died against less than 1% in Flanders and France. Estimates of Ottoman troops evacuated were at over 65,000. The most significant cause of non-battle admissions to the hospital for Allied troops was dysentery at 30,000 men.

Add another 11,000 for diarrhea, and frostbite caused over 6,600 hospitalizations, gonorrhea made up 1,800 cases, and pneumatic fever over 6,500 cases. French casualties during this campaign amounted to around 47,000; of the French casualties, 27,000 were killed, wounded, or missing, with another 20,000 having fallen sick.

There were allegations that Allied forces had bombed Ottoman hospitals and hospital ships during the start of the campaign and in September 1915. By July 1915, there were over twenty Ottoman hospitals with 10,000 beds, including three hospital ships in the area. The French government disputed these accusations through the Red Cross. The British replied that if these bombings had happened, it was purely accidental. Russian officials alleged the Ottomans had attacked two of their ships, but the Ottomans answered the vessels had been the victim of mines.

No chemical weapons were used at Gallipoli. However, the Allies debated the use throughout the campaign and transported to the theater large amounts of gas used against Ottoman troops in the Middle Eastern theater two years later during the multiple Gaza battles in 1917.

Ensuing Operations

THE ALLIED TROOPS WERE withdrawn to Lemnos and then to Egypt. French forces were combined into the Army of the Orient and then employed at Salonika. In Egypt, the British and Colonial troops from the Dardanelles, along with new divisions from the United Kingdom and Salonika, were merged into the Mediterranean Expeditionary Force and commanded by General Archibald Murray.

They joined the Egyptian forces to become the British Empire's strategic reserve, comprising thirteen mounted divisions and infantry, totaling over 400,000 men.

In March 1916, General Murray took command of both these forces and formed them into the new Egyptian Expeditionary Force and reorganized the units for service in Egypt, Europe, and elsewhere in the Middle East. The ANZAC was disbanded. The AIF (Australian Imperial Force) was enlarged with three new Australian divisions, and a New Zealand division was formed. These units were moved to the Western Front in the summer of 1916.

ANZAC SPIRIT

THE IMPORTANCE OF THE Gallipoli campaign is felt strongly in New Zealand and Australia despite only being a portion of the Allied forces. The campaign's effect was directly linked to their emergence as independent states. Over 17,000 New Zealanders and 50,000 Australians served at Gallipoli. This campaign proved significant in the emergence of a uniquely Australian identity that followed the war, closely linked to popular conceptions of the soldiers that fought during the campaign. This became embodied in the notion of the Anzac spirit.

The April 25 landing is commemorated every year in New Zealand and Australia and is known as Anzac Day. The first event was celebrated unofficially in 1916 in London, Melbourne, and Brisbane before officially being recognized as a public holiday in Australian states in 1923. Anzac Day became an official holiday in New Zealand in the 1920s. Organized marches by veterans began in 1925, the same year Dawn Service was held on the beach at Gallipoli. The first official Dawn Service took place two years later at the Sydney Cenotaph. During the 1980s, it became popular for New Zealand and Australian tourists to visit Gallipoli and attend the Dawn Service, and since then, thousands have attended.

Along with monuments and memorials built in towns and cities, buildings, streets, and public places were named after elements of the campaign, especially in Australia and New Zealand. Some examples include the Gallipoli barracks at Enoggera in Queensland and the Armed Forces armory in Corner Brook, Newfoundland, now known as the Gallipoli Armory. Gallipoli also significantly affected popular culture, including TV, film, and song. In 1971, a Scottish-born Australian folksinger named Eric Bogle wrote a famous song called "And the band played waltzing Matilda," which told the story of a young

Australian soldier maimed during the Gallipoli campaign. This song has been acclaimed for its vivid imagery from the carnage at the Gallipoli landings. To this day, it is far and wide popular, considered by some to be an antiwar song.

In modern-day Turkey, the battle is considered a significant event in the founding of a new country, although primarily remembered for the fighting near Çanakkale, where the Royal Navy was defeated in March 1915. For the Turks, March 18 is like April 25 for the New Zealanders and the Australians. Not just a public holiday, but also commemorated with Turks cherishing their martyrs at the Çanakkale Victory.

Sir Ian Hamilton

Born in January 1853, Hamilton became a British Army general with an extensive imperial British military career in the Edwardian and Victorian eras. Hamilton was recommended for the Victoria Cross twice but was deemed too young on the first occasion and too old on the second. During the first Boer War, his left hand was permanently injured, and the highlight of his career was commanding the Mediterranean Expeditionary Force in the Gallipoli campaign during World War One.

After attending the Royal Military College in Sandhurst in 1870, he received his commission by an academic exam instead of purchasing it. As soon as he was commissioned as an infantry officer, he transferred to the Gordon Highlanders after a short stint with the Suffolk Regiment. The Highlanders were an imperial garrison service in India, and on arrival, Hamilton took part in the Afghan campaign.

During the first Boer War, he was wounded at the battle of Majuba and taken prisoner by the Boers. After returning to England to recover, he was considered a war hero and even introduced to Queen Victoria. He became a captain in 1882 and took part in the Nile expedition. He led men in Burma and Bengal and was promoted to colonel after being awarded the Distinguished Service Order in 1891. In 1898, he held the post of deputy quartermaster general in India and was wounded while commanding the 3rd Brigade on the Indian frontier in Tirah.

After returning home to Britain, he was appointed commandant of the School of Musketry at Hythe.

During the second Boer War, Hamilton accompanied General White as his chief staff officer. He commanded infantry at the Battle of Elandslaagte and fought triumphantly during a massive assault at The Battle of Wagon Hill. In 1901, Hamilton was appointed military secretary at the War Office but requested to return to South Africa as the chief of staff to Commander-in-Chief Lord Kitchener.

By 1902, Hamilton was promoted to Lieutenant General Hamilton for his distinguished service and was made the military attaché of the British Indian army. He also served in Manchuria during the Russo-Japanese war. When he returned to England, he became the adjutant general to the forces in 1910.

On August 05, 1914, he was appointed the commander-in-chief of the home army. In March 1915, Kitchener appointed Hamilton, at sixty-two years old, to command the Mediterranean Expeditionary Force and take the Dardanelles Strait from the Ottomans and capture Constantinople. Hamilton was a senior and respected officer, perhaps too experienced in many campaigns, and was unconventional, too intellectual, and way too friendly with politicians to command on the Western Front.

Hamilton was not allowed to take part in the campaign's planning. Intelligence reported that the Ottoman Empire's military defensive capacity was poor and underestimated their strength. During the planning stages, the Greek army command possessed far more detailed knowledge of the Ottoman Empire's military capability than the Allies. The Greeks warned Kitchener that the British Expeditionary Force needed at least 150,000 troops to take Gallipoli; Kitchener disagreed and decided a force of 70,000 men would be more than enough to overpower any defensive garrison. After British and French warships failed to take the strait using naval power. Kitchener decided an amphibious assault on Gallipoli would be required to support the naval operations with the land campaign, and Hamilton would lead them. Hamilton then became responsible for organizing the landings. General Hamilton was given no specialized landing craft, and the troops he had been given had no training for amphibious operations.

The army's supplies were packed in ways that made them nearly impossible to access for the landings. Hamilton believed the Royal Navy would make further attacks during the campaign, realizing its likely losses. However, Allied leadership was opposed to the idea that tactical losses of ships and operations were an acceptable price, so the Allied command declined to mount another attack. With the failure of the Gallipoli campaign, Hamilton was recalled to London on October 16, 1915 ending his military career.

Hamilton spoke French, German, and Hindi. Considered kind, charming, and, while appearing frail, full of energy. He was also a prolific writer and published a poetry volume along with several novels. The opening line of his Gallipoli diary read: "There is nothing certain about war, except that one side won't win."

On October 12, 1947, at ninety-four years old, Hamilton died at his home in Hyde Park Gardens in London.

WILLIAM BIRDWOOD

Birdwood saw action in the second Boer War while serving on Lord Kitchener's staff. He commanded the ANZAC troops during Gallipoli in 1915. He led the landings on the peninsula and the evacuation later in the year before taking command of the 5th Army on the Western Front during the war's closing stages. In 1920, he commanded India's Northern Army and was then promoted to Commander-in-Chief of India in 1925.

Birdwood was born in September 1865 in India. His father was born in Bombay, educated in the UK, and went back to India after passing the Indian Civil Services Exam in 1859. Birdwood trained at the Royal Military College in Sandhurst, and after gaining an early commission because of the Russian war scare of 1885, he became a lieutenant in the Royal Lancers. From there, he joined the Bengal Staff Corps and saw action in the Tirah campaign in 1897. While serving in the second Boer War, Birdwood was a brigade major with a mounted brigade in Natal and then deputy assistant adjutant general on Kitchener's staff in October 1900. In 1902, he became Kitchener's military secretary and returned with him to Britain on board the SS *Orotava*.

When Kitchener returned to India as commander-in-chief in November 1902, Birdwood joined him as his assistant military secretary and interpreter. In October 1911, Birdwood became quartermaster general in India and a Viceroys' Legislative Council member in 1912. In 1913, he was made the secretary of the Indian Army Department.

In November 1914, Birdwood was told by Kitchener to make an army from the Australian and New Zealand troops stationed in Egypt. He was made lieutenant general and given command of the ANZAC Corps, working with General Hamilton to carry out an amphibious operation to capture Gallipoli. Birdwood and his ANZAC troops were placed under Hamilton's command. After Hamilton ordered Birdwood to land on April 25 north of Kabatepe at Anzac Cove, the ANZAC troops encountered narrow gullies, prominent ridges, dense scrub, and strong Ottoman resistance, becoming pinned down. Birdwood took command of the Australian Imperial Forces (AIF) while still commanding Allied troops on the ground in Gallipoli. He then launched a major attack against the Ottomans at the battle of Sari Bair in the August offensive, but still failed to move them off the peninsula.

He was the only core commander opposed to abandoning the Gallipoli campaign. In October 1915, he was appointed to the permanent rank of lieutenant general and took command of the newly formed Dardanelles army. Birdwood left the military service in

1930 and tried to become the governor general of Australia. He had the backing of the British government and the king, but the Australian prime minister insisted that his Australian nominee be appointed.

Birdwood returned to Gallipoli in 1936 on board the RMS *Lancastria* to visit war memorials on the peninsula before retiring from all work in 1938.

He died on May 17, 1951, and is buried at Twickenham Cemetery with full military honors. The Australian government still pays to this day for the upkeep of his grave. Many streets and public spaces in New Zealand and Australia are named or believed to be named after Birdwood; some examples are Birdwood Park in Newcastle West and a Birdwood St. in New Lambton.

Otto Liman von Sanders

Liman Von Sanders was a German Imperial Army general serving as a military advisor to the Ottoman army during the First World War.

Born Otto Viktor Karl Liman in Poland in 1855 to wealthy parents, Liman entered the army in 1874. In 1878, he attended the Military Academy in Berlin and was appointed as a squadron commander in 1891. He was ennobled in June 1913 and chose his late wife's maiden name, von Sanders, as his nobiliary suffix. In German literature, his proper surname is

Liman, but in English works, he is better known as Sanders.

Like other Prussian generals prior to him, such as Goltz and Moltke, Sanders was appointed the head of the German military mission to the Ottoman Empire. The Ottomans had been trying to upgrade their army to European standards for over eighty years. Sanders was the last German officer to attempt this task. In 1914, before the outbreak of the war in Europe, the Ottomans allied with Germany against Russia. However, this alliance did not force them to take military action, and on October 31, 1914, the Ottomans officially joined the war on Germany and Austria-Hungary's side.

Britain and France waited until November 5 to officially declare war.

When the Allies' initial attempt to force the Dardanelles by sea failed in March 1915 in the Gallipoli campaign, it was because of gunfire coming from Ottoman forts on both sides of the strait. This caused the Allies to attempt an amphibious assault and capture the forts to clear the strait, leading to the battle of Gallipoli. Sanders had little time to organize the defenses, but he had the Ottoman 5th Army (the best army the Ottomans had) on the Gallipoli peninsula. Sanders had six divisions with 84,000 well-equipped soldiers. He was also helped by poor allied leadership. When the British landed a significant force at Cape Helles in April 1915, he pulled back his strong defenses on the coast. The local Ottoman commanders moved troops and defenses inland to prepare for an allied attack.

One of Sanders's best decisions during this time was to promote Mustafa Kemal to command his 19th Division. Kemal's division was crucial to the Ottoman's defenses. His troops occupied a ridgeline over the ANZAC landing site just as the troops were moving up the slope. Kemal's troops were never forced off the ridge for the next five months, even after ANZAC troops tried another amphibious assault at Suvla Bay. The Ottoman defenders repelled that attack as well; the only bright spot for the British through the entire campaign was that they could evacuate their positions with little loss. In the end, this battle was a significant victory for the Ottoman army, and some credit must be given to the generalship of Sanders.

After Gallipoli, Sanders was sent to fight the British in Mesopotamia. In 1918, during the last year of the war, Sanders took command of the Ottoman army during the Palestine and Sinai campaign, replacing German general Erich Falkenhayn, who had been defeated by the British at the end of 1917. The decline of power in the Ottoman army frustrated Sanders. His forces were weakened and unable to do anything else than occupy defensive positions and wait for the British to attack. When the Allies finally unleashed their army, the entire Ottoman army was destroyed in a week of fighting at the battle of Megiddo.

During the battle, Sanders was nearly captured by Allied troops. He was accused of war crimes. The British alleged he deported over 35,000 Greeks under horrible conditions and was responsible for the partial assassination of over 300,000 Ottoman Greeks under his authority. Sanders was also blamed for deliberately cutting a trench system through war cemeteries at Gallipoli and the mistreatment of British POWs. In 1919, he was arrested for war crimes for sanctioning the Greek and Armenian massacres, but only spent six months in a prison in Malta before being released. After his time in Malta, Sanders returned home and retired from the German army.

In 1927, he published a book called "Five years in Turkey," which he'd written in captivity in Malta about his experiences during the war. Sanders died in August 1929 in Munich at seventy-four years old.

Mustafa Kemal Atatürk

Kemal was a revolutionary leader and founding father of the Republic of Turkey. He served as its first president from 1923 until 1938. He modernized Turkey into an industrialized and secular nation. Because of his political and military accomplishments, Kemal was one of the most significant political leaders of the twentieth century.

Kemal was distinguished for securing an Ottoman victory during the Gallipoli campaign. After the

Ottoman Empire's dissolution, he led the Turkish national movement and resisted Turkey's partition from the conquering Allied powers. He established a provisional government in Ankara and defeated forces sent by the Allies, emerging victorious from what was later known as the Turkish war of independence.

He also abolished the decrepit Ottoman Empire and founded the Turkish Republic to replace it. Kemal began a new economic, political, and cultural reform program to build a secular and modern progressive nation-state. He made primary education mandatory and free and opened thousands of schools across the country. He introduced a Latin-based Turkish alphabet to replace the old Ottoman alphabet and granted women equal political and civil rights during his presidency.

He created a government under a Turkification policy that unified a secular nation under the Turkish banner. Under Kemal's presidency, all minorities in Turkey were asked to speak Turkish in public but were allowed to maintain their languages in private. The Turkish parliament granted him the name "father of the Turks" in 1934. Kamal died in November 1938 at Dolmabahçe Palace in Istanbul. He was fifty-seven years old.

Author's Note

Thanks for reading this short history of Gallipoli. If you'd leave a review or rating, I'd appreciate it. Also, if you'd like get my newest releases first and free, enter your email below.

AUTHOR'S NOTE

MILITARY HISTORY BOOKS

Get Free History Books

Enter Your email to get FREE eBooks and audiobooks delivered to your inbox. No Spam. No BS. Just free military history books.

Email

Sign Me Up

Printed in Great Britain
by Amazon